PORTRAIT OF
MORECAMBE BAY

JON SPARKS

HALSGROVE

First published in Great Britain in 2008

Title page photograph: Clock Tower, Morecambe

British Library Cataloguing-in-Publication Data
A CIP record for this title is available from the British Library

ISBN 978 1 84114 602 7

HALSGROVE
Halsgrove House
Ryelands Industrial Estate
Bagley Road, Wellington
Somerset TA21 9PZ
T: 0823 653777
F: 01823 216796
email: sales@halsgrove.com
website: www.halsgrove.com

Printed by D'Auria Industrie Grafiche Spa, Italy

INTRODUCTION

Nothing sums up the magic of Morecambe Bay more swiftly than the short train journey from Arnside to Grange-over-Sands. Leaving the station, the train booms across the old iron viaduct and you don't know which way to look. North, the Kent Estuary mirrors Whitbarrow's limestone ridge and, beyond that, the high Lakeland fells. Shelduck and redshank forage, indifferent to the view or the train. Then, as you approach Grange, the scale expands, the sweep of the Bay itself opening to the south. Limestone knolls punctuate the panorama. It is five minutes of magic and there is no road journey that can compete with it. In fact the whole of the train journey from Lancaster to Ulverston is a classic. Arnside to Grange is merely the jewel in the crown.

What is it that's so special about Morecambe Bay? I've known it most of my life, photographed it intensively, walked its shores and its sands, climbed its crags, and I still struggle to encapsulate it in a few lines.

The bald facts are clear enough. It is the second largest bay in the UK, after the Wash, but has the greatest area of intertidal sands and mudflats – over 300 square kilometres. It is of international importance for wildlife of many kinds, especially migrating birds. But that is only part of the story. They say nothing of the dynamism of this landscape, from the twice-daily tides to the ceaseless shifting of sandbanks and channels, the advance and retreat of the salt-marsh, and the endlessly varied play of light across these reflective surfaces.

In its widest sense, the Bay is bounded by a line drawn from Fleetwood to Barrow. But the towns which wholly belong to the Bay are Ulverston, Morecambe and Heysham. Indeed it is possible to speak of an 'inner' bay. A simple definition of this would be given by a line from Heysham Head to Humphrey Head, but it would be a shame to exclude Ulverston. What is fairly clear to me is that most of the best scenery is concentrated towards this inner reach, with the magnificent Leven Sands and the Kent Estuary overlooked by hills like Hampsfell, Arnside Knott and Warton Crag.

Warton Crag is hard to beat for an overview of the 'inner' Bay; for the broader picture there's nowhere better than Lancaster's Ashton Memorial. But the quintessential Morecambe Bay panorama is surely that from Morecambe itself. Morecambe – which takes its name from the Bay, not the other way around – may have outlived its glory days, but nothing can take away that view, and there's justice in its claim to have the best sunsets in the world. They can be marvellous at any time of year, but are probably at their absolute best in high summer, when the sun sinks behind the Lakeland fells.

Of course there is much more to the Bay than broad views, grand though they are. In winter, wildfowl and waders descend in their tens of thousands, following the tides in and out. The visual impact is matched by the many-layered soundscapes, with the honking of geese, the shrill peeping of oyster-catchers and possibly the loveliest sound on Earth, the bubbling call of the curlew.

The Bay's landscapes are also many-layered and exist on many scales. Miniature canyons and meandering creeks form in the sand and mud, to be reshaped with every tide. Human footpaths wind around the shore while invertebrates sketch their trails across a single stone. The Bay is both intimate and infinite. It is also fragile and irreplaceable.

Fragile it may be, but the Bay can also be dangerous. Its mobile sands and fast-advancing tides have claimed countless lives over the centuries. Morecambe Bay remains a wild place.

Jon Sparks

The Kent Estuary from Sandside
The Kent is one of the main rivers flowing into the Bay. The limestone ridge of
Whitbarrow Scar rises on the far side, with a snowy Lakeland skyline beyond.

Morecambe Bay from Williamson Park
Lancaster's Williamson Park is perfectly situated to give
panoramic views over the Bay, and on high summer evenings
the sun sets behind the Lakeland fells.

Sunset and Arnside Tower
Looking across Silverdale Moss to Arnside Tower, with the
lower slopes of Arnside Knott on the right.

Shoreline near Bardsea
A view along the shoreline at Bardsea, near Ulverston,
from the aptly-named Sea Wood.

Herons, Arnside
I was setting up to take a shot of the reflections and silhouetted hills
beyond before I even realised that there were seven herons in shot.

Poulton College, Morecambe
Poulton College is a listed
building and a familiar
landmark in Morecambe;
the sailing-ship weather-
vane, however is a feature
that not everyone notices.

Stone circle, Birkrigg Common
The area round Birkrigg Common, just south of Ulverston, has been
occupied for millennia; this circle is reckoned to date from the Bronze
Age. It is locally known as the Druid's Circle. There are various theories
about the purpose of stone circles; one that has not yet gained wide
support is that they are simply an early form of view indicator.

Waves, Silverdale Shore
That Morecambe Bay is a dynamic landscape is a truism, but it's
most obvious on days like this when you can see the saltmarsh
disappearing before your eyes.

Channels, looking towards Humphrey Head
Once on a Cross-Bay Walk my partner overheard someone remark incredulously,
'there's a man over there taking pictures of mud'. Well, here's a picture of mud,
albeit taken on a different occasion.

Eric Morecambe Stage, evening
An unusual angle on the Eric
Morecambe 'Stage', taken
from a 'cherry-picker' shortly
after the statue's unveiling.

Morecambe Bay sunset
Morecambe Bay is justly renowned for its sunsets, but I've
never seen a more colourful example than this.

Looking towards Heysham Head
Heysham lies just south of
Morecambe and today is part
of one conurbation, but its
sandstone headland gives it
an elevation advantage over
its low-lying neighbour.

Towards Moat Scar
Moat Scar is on the Furness coast and there is indeed a motte on the crest.
I only had a couple of minutes to take this shot as the tide was advancing.

Eric Morecambe Hide, Leighton Moss
The RSPB reserve at Leighton Moss is centred on freshwater
wetlands but also has a couple of hides overlooking the saltmarsh
and tidal pools on the edge of the Bay.

Sunset over saltmarsh
Seen from high on Warton Crag, this
is the same area of saltmarsh which
belongs to the reserve.

Walker, Arnside Park
Arnside Park is typical of the deciduous woodlands which still fringe
much of the shoreline, particularly of the 'inner bay'.

Fields, near Pilling
These fields lie a short way east of the Lane End's amenity area. The photo is
taken from the embankment which protects them from the sea.

Heysham Village
Tucked into the shelter of
Heysham Head, the old core
of the village still retains
much of its character.

Cottage, Poulton

Poulton ('by the sands') is the original village which predates the town of Morecambe. The town really grew up in the nineteenth century around the railway station, and took its name from the Bay rather than the reverse.

Fairy Steps
The 'Fairy Steps' themselves are hidden in the narrow cleft which can
be seen below the yew tree towards the right of the picture. The cleft
is extremely narrow; legend has it that if you can negotiate it
without touching the sides, the fairies will grant you a wish.
I suspect they are rarely required to pay up.

Approaching snowstorm, Red Hills
A far from promising winter's day yielded dramatic lighting
as the sun sneaked between bands of cloud.

Piel and Roa Islands
Piel and Roa Islands are just south of Barrow-in-Furness. Piel Island,
with its castle, is a true island, reached only by boat, but Roa Island is
linked to the mainland by a causeway.

Evening, Sandside
Sandside – a perfectly descriptive name – is a small village
beside the Kent Estuary, upstream from Arnside.

Morecambe Bay from above Cark
One of the best walks in the hinterland of the Bay is from Cark to
Grange via Cartmel and Hampsfell. This is the first view back over the
Bay as the route climbs above Cark.

Clouds over the Bay
On this occasion there were so many different layers of cloud that
it was almost disorientating, with no clear horizon.

Pebbles, Walney Island
The shores of the Bay are usually sandy, not stony, but Walney Island lies
on the outer edge, where the bay meets the Irish Sea, and stones are
swept down from the West Cumbria coast.

Spring foliage, Arnside Knott
Fresh young leaves of ash and hazel contrast with the dark evergreen pine.

Hest Bank Jetty
This is a great example of the dynamic nature of the bay. The old jetty at
Hest Bank was hidden by the sands for decades and its existence was
largely forgotten until it was revealed by shifting sands in 2006.

The Stone Jetty
The Stone Jetty is the real centrepiece of Morecambe's promenade,
and has been transformed by the TERN project into a showcase
of public art, with mazes and games among the features.

Cross-Bay walkers
A small group of walkers reflected in the watery ground. In the distance is Humphrey Head.

Looking towards Aldingham
Aldingham is on the Furness shore; just a few houses and an attractive church.

Piel Island from Walney Island
Piel Castle was built in the fourteenth century for the Abbots
of Furness, serving them occasionally as a refuge and more
regularly to control maritime traffic.

The Stone Jetty and Coniston Fells
Once, Morecambe's Stone Jetty was the place where fresh Morecambe Bay shrimp
were loaded onto express trains for rapid transport to metropolitan breakfast tables.
Today's trains stop a few hundred metres inland.

Eric Morecambe
Graham Ibbeson's statue is just a fraction larger than life, which seems appropriate. Eric, one of Britain's best-loved comedians, was born Eric Bartholomew but took his stage name from his home town.

Bird-watchers, Leighton Moss
The most luxurious of Leighton's half-dozen hides gives
a broad view of the reserve's meres and reed-beds.

Wind turbines, from Walney Island
With its tidal shallows, low shorelines and fragile ecosystems,
Morecambe Bay would be greatly affected by any marked rise
in sea levels, so it is as good a place as any to ponder on global
warming and renewable energy.

Walkers, from Heald Brow
This embankment stretching from Crag Foot to Heald Brow dates from the eighteenth century and divides drained pasture on the left from unreclaimed saltmarsh on the right.

Furness Abbey
Strikingly constructed of red sandstone, Furness Abbey is a Cistercian foundation dating back to the thirteenth century. It lies in a sheltered and often shady valley just outside Dalton-in-Furness.

Cark
This row of cottages overlooks the River Eea
at Cark, on the Cartmel peninsula.

Summer evening, Morecambe
A relaxed evening atmosphere near the Eric Morecambe Stage.

Fishing boats, Morecambe
Fine early morning light. The distant
hill is Arnside Knott.

Woods, Fairy Steps
Fairy Steps has a fine variety of woodland, with stands of tall pine,
and mixed deciduous woods as well as these yews.

Saltmarsh patterns
It's much easier to plot a route through the maze of channels
from up high than when you're at ground level.

Train at Crag Foot
The rail journey round the Bay is an essential Morecambe Bay
experience, offering a far more scenic journey than anything available by
road. Between Carnforth and Silverdale, the train gives good views
of the Crag Foot wetlands while on the other side are tidal pools,
saltmarsh, and the vastness of the Bay itself.

Ferry at Fleetwood
Fleetwood's Queen's Terrace is seen across the mouth of the
Wyre from Knott End. Ferries run twice daily from
Fleetwood to Larne in Northern Ireland.

Cottages, Sunderland
According to the Ordnance Survey, the name of the village at the mouth of the Lune Estuary is Sunderland, and Sunderland Point is the actual headland a kilometre or so to the south. However, everyone locally refers to the village too as Sunderland Point. Its single access road is still regularly flooded by high tides.

Climbers, Jack Scout
Known to climbers as Jack Scout Cove, these cliffs overlook the inlet of
Cow's Mouth. Along with Humphrey Head, which has some much
harder routes, this is the only cliff on the Bay of real interest to climbers.

Sign and gate, Silverdale
A short walk links The Cove and
The Shore at Silverdale, and this gate
gives access to the elevated path
across The Lots for the return leg.

Cross-Bay Walk
The historic Cross-Bay route was from Hest Bank to Kent's Bank,
but shifting channels have made this difficult and the
standard route today starts from Arnside. Here a group
of walkers is crossing the main Kent channel.

Rampside Light
The Rampside Light is the sole survivor of over a dozen light-houses which once safeguarded the approaches to Barrow. It too was threatened with demolition but local people campaigned to have it listed as a historic monument. Piel and Roa Islands can be just be seen through the mist.

Winter evening, from Arnside Knott
Arnside Knott is a fantastic viewpoint and this is one of the best slices of that panorama,
looking over the Kent Estuary to Whitbarrow Scar and the skyline of the Lakeland Fells.

Searchlight emplacement, Walney Island
This is part of First World War defences on Walney's western shore.

Beach detail, near Newbiggin
Newbiggin is a small settlement on the
shore of the Furness peninsula.

Evening, Morecambe
Blazing sunsets are certainly a
Morecambe Bay speciality but it's
nearly always worth lingering after
the sun has dipped below the
horizon, as the colours can be more
subtle but just as attractive.

Hazel catkins and limestone pavement
Around most of the Bay, the underlying rock is Carboniferous limestone
and hazel is one of its typical trees.

Driftwood and Chapel Island
Chapel Island lies in the Leven Estuary, just below Ulverston.
Beyond is the Cartmel peninsula.

Mother and Child
Shane Johnstone's exhilarating sculpture enjoys a prominent and breezy
position at Scalestones Point, between Morecambe and Hest Bank.

Cartmel Priory
Cartmel may lie a few kilometres inland but it has strong historical associations with the cross-bay trade route and within the mediaeval priory church are a number of poignant memorials to people who perished on the treacherous crossing.

Morecambe Bay from Humphrey Head
Humphrey Head gives what must be one of the great short walks (a couple of kilometres
at most). It's best at a low-ish tide as a circular route is then possible.

Sea-campion
Sea-campion, as its name suggests, is a typical flower of rocky shorelines, though it is also found on inland cliffs in the Lake District.

Evening, on Warton Crag
Warton Crag is an important nature reserve with a rich flora, but for
many the biggest attraction is its expansive views, here looking west past
Gibraltar Point to Humphrey Head.

Heysham Head
Heysham Head is one of the handful of places around the Bay where the
rock is sandstone rather than the more usual limestone.

Tracks on stone
There's always something to see between the tides, and
here it was this dense network of tracks on the stones.

Cormorants, Stone Jetty
These sculptures nicely capture the
characteristic posture which
cormorants adopt to dry their wings.

Oystercatchers, near Aldingham
Oystercatchers are among the commonest birds along the coast, but they
are notably skittish. They are also, for their size, some of the noisiest.

Clock Tower, Morecambe
The Clock Tower, dating from 1905, is one of
Morecambe's best-loved landmarks.

Winter evening, Arnside
A view looking down on Arnside and the Kent Estuary beyond;
a stretch of the railway embankment can be seen.

Sea anglers, Sandylands
It was a very pleasant day to be out on the Prom, but I didn't see
anyone catching anything. The Isle of Man ferry can be seen
in the distance on its way out from Heysham.

Piel and Roa Islands from Foulney Island
Foulney Island is just a low, sandy spit but a very important
site for nesting birds and is now a nature reserve.

Nets in the Bay
I believe these nets were there to catch flukes (flounders). I got
my knees and elbows muddy in pursuit of a low enough angle.

Trailer, near Humphrey Head
Ancient tractors and trailers are favoured
by the cockle-fishers around the bay.
A section of the cliffs of Humphrey
Head can be seen behind.

Ulverston Canal
The Ulverston Canal was said to be the shortest, widest
and deepest canal in the country at the time of its
construction in the late eighteenth century.

Star map, Morecambe
The punning connection between stars and
starfish is typical of the light-hearted nature of
Morecambe's TERN Project artworks.

Walker on saltmarsh
The springy turf of the saltmarsh
is a delight to walk on, but threading
the maze of channels can make
routes tortuous.

Between tides, Cow's Mouth
Bare feet are best when venturing out after a falling tide, and on hot
days in particular there's a sensuous pleasure in mud between your toes.

Sambo's Grave
Sambo's Grave is a poignant spot at which to recall that 2007, the year of publication, marks the 200th anniversary of the abolition of the slave trade in the British Empire. It also serves as a reminder that the port of Lancaster grew rich on the proceeds of this terrible trade. The grave lies just outside the village of Sunderland, looking west over the sea.

Flower-meadows, Heathwaite
It takes careful management of grazing (not least the depredations
of rabbits!) to maintain a herb-rich meadow like this.

Driftwood, Walney Island
A substantial piece of driftwood on the western shore of Walney Island.

Jenny Brown's Point
This wind-sculpted hawthorn is at Jenny Brown's Point, near Silverdale.

The Leven Estuary
The River Leven, which flows out of Windermere, is only about 7km long
(to the tidal limit), but has a substantial estuary. Like the Kent, it is crossed
by a railway viaduct well downstream of any road crossing.

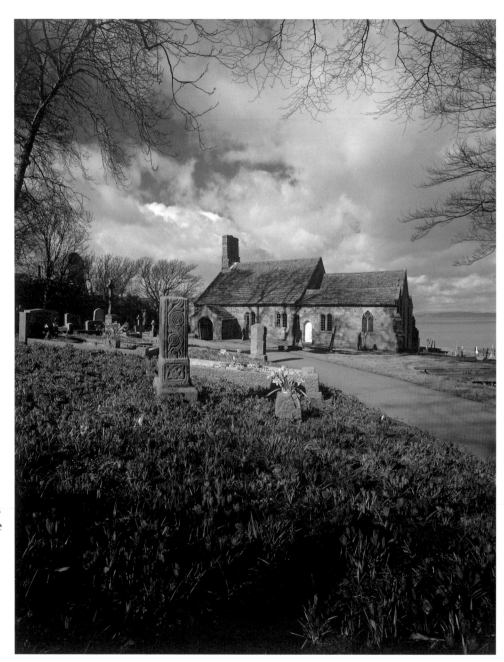

St Peter's church, Heysham
The ancient church at Heysham has few rivals around the Bay, and none when it comes to producing a crop of crocuses each spring.

The Pepper-pot and Silverdale
A short climb through Eaves Wood leads to the Pepper-pot. Part of Silverdale
village is seen below, and in the distance are the Bowland Fells.

Tractor in the Bay
Old tractors still have an edge over modern four-wheel drives in the shifting landscape of the Bay. This one is on safety duty during a Cross-Bay Walk.

Cross-Bay ride
As the traditional route, the Bay crossing was in regular use by horses,
coaches and foot traffic, but today this is a rare sight.

Child with bucket
This child didn't care that
Morecambe's beach was a bit
muddy. This struck me as a
moment of pure, uncomplicated joy.

Breakwater detail
Weathered timber, green algae and raking winter light
combined to create textures which fascinated me.

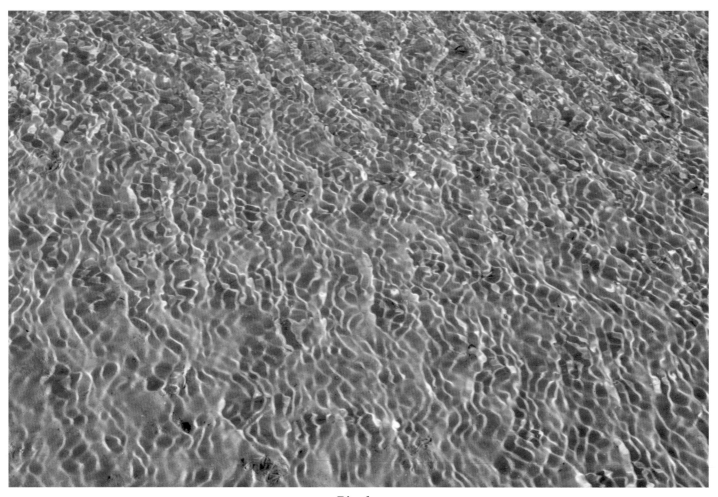

Ripples
It was the interaction of the ripples on the water with the
rippled sand underneath that caught my eye here.

Yacht and young angler, Morecambe
It should perhaps be noted that there are numerous warning notices advising people not to venture onto the boulders of Morecambe's sea defences.

Cloudy day, looking towards Humphrey Head
The reflective sands and channels of the Bay make
the most of even the slightest glimmer of sun.

Whitebeam, Park Point
Morecambe Bay even has its own tree, a subspecies
of whitebeam found nowhere else.

Summit of Clougha Pike
For a broad view of the Bay you need a high viewpoint and arguably the best is Clougha Pike,
in the Forest of Bowland, 413m high and just 10km from the nearest point on the shoreline.

Morecambe Golf Club
Personally I'm inclined to agree with Mark Twain's dictum that 'golf is a
good walk spoiled', but surely all can agree that with Morecambe Bay
for a backdrop, it will be a very good walk.

St Patrick's Chapel, Heysham Head
The ruins on Heysham Head date back to Saxon times and legend
maintains that it was here that St Patrick first landed on his
mission to bring Christianity to England.

Frosty morning, Silverdale Moss
Silverdale Moss is a puzzling name as it is actually closer to Arnside.
It is representative of the low-lying terrain which forms large tracts of
the hinterland around the Bay and much of which has either never
been drained or has reverted to wetland.

Piel and Roa Islands from Beacon Hill
Part of the Roa Island causeway can be seen on the left and in
the foreground the shimmering expanse of Concle Sands.

Lichenous stones, Walney Island
Lichens are slow-growing and are generally taken to be a good
indicator of air-quality. The southern tip of Walney Island is now a
nature reserve, but the middle part of the island is an urbanised
offshoot of Barrow-in-Furness.

Reeds, Leighton Moss
The reed-beds of Leighton Moss are home to many species
of bird, most notably bitterns and bearded tits.

Ulverston from from Birkrigg Common
Birkrigg Common is the most westerly and the gentlest of the
limestone ridges which punctuate the landscape around the Bay.
It offers easy walking and great sea views, while in the other
direction the Coniston Fells are about 25km away.

Sunset over Leighton Moss
This combination of rising mist and a colourful sunset caught
me by surprise and I had to shoot quickly, from more or
less the spot where I first saw the phenomenon.

Walkers on the sands
At low tide there is a choice for walkers at many places along the shore
(this is Park Point, near Arnside). An obvious stratagem is to walk one
way on the sands and back along the cliff-top; and if the tide has come
in in the interim, it will feel like a completely different walk.

Old breakwater, near Sunderland Point
This is located on the inland side of the point,
a short way up the Lune Estuary.

Grange-over-Sands from The Lots, Silverdale
Grange is one of the main settlements on the shores of the Bay.
Though technically on the west coast, it faces east, its
sheltered position giving it an exceptionally mild climate.

Lighthouse, Lune Estuary
This little lighthouse near Cockersands Abbey marks one side of the
deep-water channel in the Lune Estuary. Beyond is the southern shore
of the Bay between Pilling and Knott End.

Low tide, on the Furness Shore
A main road tracks almost the entire length of the Furness shoreline from
Rampside to Ulverston. Walkers following the Cumbria Coastal way can
go one better, and stay with the shoreline throughout.

Arnside Tower
Around the Bay are several pele towers, a form of fortified manor-house
dating from the middle ages. Arnside Tower is one of the largest and
most striking but in a ruinous state and considered unsafe to enter.

Walney Lighthouse
Walney Lighthouse is an important landmark for shipping
to this day as Barrow remains an active port.

Reeds, Leighton Moss
A perfectly still evening produced perfect reflections.

Greenodd Sands from Park Head
It was an overcast day and starting to rain, but I almost felt
that this enhanced the vastness of the sands.

Mural, Poulton
This mural painting on a cottage in Poulton, Morecambe, depicts traditional methods of cockle-harvesting in the Bay.

Flight of waders, from Heysham Head
In the distance (about 40km away in fact) are the Coniston Fells.

Paraglider, Morecambe
I'd come to photograph the sunset but the sight of a powered paraglider
cruising slowly along just offshore added an extra element.

Wild daffodils, Far Arnside
These are real wild daffodils, smaller and more delicate than garden
varieties. Tragically, in some places they are now being displaced by the
(no doubt well-intentioned) practice of planting garden varieties on
verges and in other places well beyond gardens.

Footpath sign, Crag Foot
The Lancashire Coastal Way is a 220km trail. I suspect it's rarely walked
as a continuous whole, but many stretches are deservedly popular.

The Leven Estuary, morning
Mist clears slowly from the sands of the Leven Estuary on a morning of
perfect calm. The impression of peace is purely visual, however, as the
A592 runs no more than 100m from the location.

Piel and Roa Islands from Concle
Piel Island is served by a regular ferry only at weekends, but has its own pub.

Yew trees, Arnside Knott
Yew is one of the characteristic trees of the limestone areas, but this
grove is one of the best. On this particular day it was not hard
to see why the yew has such mystical significance.

Limestone pavements, Cow's Mouth
Cow's Mouth is so called, apparently, because it was where
cattle were driven ashore after crossing the Bay.

Winter walk, Warton Crag
The summit of Warton Crag is the site of an Iron Age hill-fort, though
only an expert eye will detect much evidence of it today.

Stormy light, Kent Estuary
This metallic light – looking from Sandside towards Arnside –
was soon swallowed by the approaching clouds.

Sunset, Cockersands
Low tide lays bare the New Red Sandstone rocks at Cockersands. At high
tide little is seen of them. The same rock forms low cliffs at Heysham Head
and is also encountered in the Furness peninsula.

Bird-watchers, Silverdale shore
Morecambe Bay is internationally important for bird life,
especially winter visitors and passage migrants, and
therefore naturally attracts many bird-watchers as well.

Hotels, Morecambe
The 6km of Morecambe Promenade is lined for most of its length by
hotels and guest-houses, testifying to its historic importance as a
coastal resort. Direct rail links to West Yorkshire led to it
being dubbed 'Bradford by the Sea'.

Fishing boat and and Coniston Fells
Fishing, mostly for shrimp, is still carried out on a small scale in
Morecambe, though Fleetwood is the main port.

Anglers, Arnside
Patience and warm clothing seem to be the main requisites for the sea
angler; rather like landscape photography, really.

Winter view from Warton Crag
This slice of the view takes in Trowbarrow Quarry, near Silverdale,
the Kent Estuary, Whitbarrow Scar and the Lakeland heights
of Fairfield and Helvellyn.

Crab sculpture, Morecambe Promenade
All along Morecambe Promenade, a wide range of art works, themed around the wildlife of the Bay, vie for attention with the panorama of the Bay itself.

The Kent Estuary from Haverbrack Bank
Haverbrack Bank, near Milnthorpe, is not one of the better-known
viewpoints around the Bay, but there's no better place to appreciate the
sweeping curves of the inner reaches of the Kent Estuary.

Sheep on Meathop Marsh
It's reckoned that saltmarsh lamb has a superior flavour – perhaps it's the salt.
Arnside and the Knott can be seen in the background.

Low tide, Humphrey Head
It was fascinating to explore the pools around the tip of Humphrey Head,
but it would be a bad place to get caught by a rising tide.

Arnside and the Knott
There's a pleasing unity about Arnside, its rows of limestone-built
Victorian houses making it probably the most graceful village on the Bay.

Bardsea from Birkrigg Common
A view over the village, with the spire of Holy Trinity Church.
Beyond is Chapel Island in the Leven Estuary and the
hills of the Cartmel peninsula.

Windsurfer, Morecambe
Morecambe may not be noted
as a great windsurfing centre but on
the right day can provide perfect
conditions.

Channels, evening
This is a perfect example of what makes Morecambe Bay inexhaustible
for the photographer. This shot can never be repeated; come back the
next day and not only the light but the state of the tide will be different,
and there will always be small shifts in some of the channels too.

Cottages, Ulverston
Ulverston is a lively and interesting place but, like most towns,
blighted by too much traffic. A proper pedestrian scheme
could give it a real boost.

Homecoming trawler, Fleetwood
It's often overlooked that Fleetwood has a foothold on
Morecambe Bay. This sculpture marks the spot where
families would watch for the safe return of loved ones.

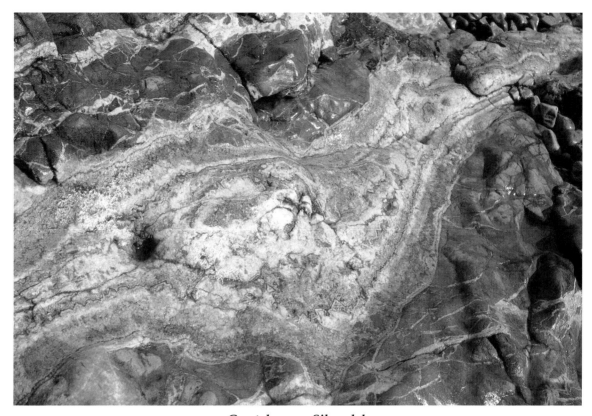

Crystals, near Silverdale
Calcite crystals and haematite staining create unusual colours
and textures in the limestone rocks.

Rough seas, Morecambe
Shallow and relatively sheltered,
Morecambe Bay does not often see
huge seas but the combination of a
high tide and onshore wind can
still produce big waves.

Arnside Knott, evening
It's the northward panorama from Arnside Knott that usually grabs attention,
but there are also places which give fine views south from
Arnside Knott over Silverdale towards Morecambe and Heysham.

Cloud inversion, Arnside Knott
Arnside Knott is only 159m high, so it's fairly unusual to climb above
the clouds, but all the more memorable for that.

Evening roost
A flock of lapwings settle for the evening, seen from one of
the hides on the seaward side of Leighton Moss.